To Helen &

family

With Love xx

Diversity Acrostic Poem

Diversity Acrostic Poem

1st Edition 2021

Cover design by Timi Phillips (@artby_timi)

Published by VOT Training

www.vottraining.co.uk

Printed in Great Britain

ISBN 978-1-8384441-0-5

Diversity Acrostic Poem

Working with Diversity & Developing Culturally Sensitive Practice in Social Work and Social Care

Vivian Okeze – Tirado

Published by VOT Training

Table of Contents

Diversity is the norm in nature. Being part of a minority is being part of the whole.

***

Prologue

The murder in broad daylight of an unarmed black man in the United States, George Floyd, in May 2020, stirred me to put all aside to complete this book. This book is based on the Diversity Acrostic poem I produced in 2015. I created this poem by utilising the word diversity and reproducing phrases that best describe the act of working with difference and becoming a culturally sensitive practitioner. This book essentially elaborates on the poem and supports good Social Work and Social Care practice in this area. Through this book, I hope to advocate for Justice and Equality, Anti-oppressive and Anti-discriminatory Social Work practice, and the embrace of Diversity & Inclusion in our Society. I will focus on cultural difference and anti-racist practice following the tense racial climate at the time of writing in 2020 and the Black Lives Matter movement's prominence. This book's content will help develop cultural competence skills in Social care. The premise is that racism is entrenched in our Society, be it conscious, unconscious, or institutional. Therefore, it is only logical that in trying to combat it, one must look at it from the perspective of impacting institutional learning.

The Diversity Acrostic Poem book is an educational resource written not just for Social work & Social care staff but also for individuals seeking knowledge around diversity and cultural competence. It is also beneficial for Government officials who formulate policies for citizens, including vulnerable citizens. They also directly engage with the public face-to-face and through the media. These officials need the enablement to engage with a diverse society confidently. This book will help readers undertake a systematic self-analysis around the Equality Act 2010 protected characteristics. It will also help identify barriers to working with diversity and promote inclusion in our Society. Social workers sign up to promote social change and social justice. The ethos of justice and equality are a core aspect of social work training and practice. Social workers are trained to acknowledge and respect diversity, to recognise and challenge oppression and discrimination in their work. In recent years, there have been questions around whether Social work training enhances this ethos or whether the teaching itself could be oppressive. Chief Social Worker for Children and Families Isabelle Trowler, in July 2020, wrote to Social Work England's chief executive urging him to address "serious concerns" from students over a lack of focus on anti-discriminatory practice. Universities are being called upon to embed teaching on white privilege and fragility in anti-racist training, which is optimistic.

Bearing in mind that social work and social care staff are busy professionals, I have made this book concise and to the point. Each acrostic poem's dimension represents a chapter of the book and is introduced with a pictorial. One of the poem's dimensions includes interesting personal anecdotes with humour elements that I hope readers will find amusing yet educational. The book begins with an open letter to all, which paid tribute to George Floyd, published in the West Sussex County Times in June 2020. I have also ended the book with a brief note to readers. I hope that this book will serve as a practical tool of learning to awaken racial consciousness and arouse empathy for the plight of black and ethnic minority groups in a world where white privilege is very perceptible. The poem creates reflective discourse and supports working with the vulnerable and the less privileged to make a difference. The reflection pages at the end of the book will help readers make some notes to support their learning.

As a human being and a social work practitioner in the tense racial climate at the time of writing, I did not want to sit back and do nothing because it would not be the right thing. It is often said that success is not only what you accomplish but what you can motivate others to do.

I hope that this book: Diversity Acrostic Poem (Working with Diversity & Developing Culturally Sensitive Practice in Social Work and Social Care), encourages readers to connect to the plight of the less privileged in our Society and make a difference.

***

Author's Note

George Floyd - A call for Justice and Equality – An open letter to all ... By Vivian Okeze – Tirado. (Published in the West Sussex County Times June 18, 2020).

Dear all,

I hope this letter meets you all well. I would like to lend my voice concerning the gruesome murder in broad daylight of a fellow human being, an unarmed black man George Floyd in the US seen as an act of racism all around the World. This event affects us all because it is a painful wound to humanity. The video, as widely shown, is quite distressing & saddening to watch. No human being should have to undergo such treatment regardless of their race, colour, religion, sex, etc... Such display of racial injustice and inequality is not an isolated incident but has been ongoing for decades, not just in the US but all over the western World / Europe, etc. A systematic degradation, covert and overt discrimination, plundering, limitation, restrictions, etc.

To those who think that the recent anti-racism protests have gone on long enough, the question is; what is being done or proposed by the Leaders in terms of reforms and policies to create real, lasting change around this issue? Racism cannot continue to be ignored. Folks, standing aside or assuming ignorance is no longer an option. We can now see that the three police officers who stood by, watched, and did nothing during the murder of George Floyd are now facing charges of accomplices to murder. This is what happens when we stand by and do nothing amid oppression and injustice — a lesson to be learnt by all.

To those who say that George Floyd was a "criminal ". What happened to "innocent until proven guilty?". Are criminals now meant to be killed gruesomely on the streets by Law enforcement agents? Also, is there any human being who can testify to doing no wrong in their lifetime? Whatever that wrong would have looked like! People have a right to turn their life around without prejudice or judgement or people digging up their past at the slightest provocation, particularly when they are of a certain race.

The worldwide protests & mixed protesters from all walks of life, all cultures, all colours, etc..., all around the World shows that there is hope yet. It means that there are humanitarian people out there who can recognise injustice, show love and solidarity to one another, and even risk their lives doing so for justice and equality.

There is hope yet...

Where does hope lie…?

The ball is now in the court for our leaders, powerful individuals, and groups to create positive change once and for all. No more hypocrisy, no more distraction tactics or lip service, no more political correctness, or well-drafted diplomatic speeches. Enough is enough. We are all involved. We are all connected; we need each other; let us refrain from feeling threatened and embrace diversity with all positivity.

If you ever need to know how connected we all are, please refer to the recent Covid 19 pandemic, which effectively spread rapidly from country to country, person to person regardless of class, race, gender, colour, rich, poor, powerful, or non-powerful, etc.

If you are still feeling detached about the plight of Black & BAME and Black Lives Matter, please go and watch the film "The Boy in the striped pyjamas" based on the novel by John Boyne 2006. In this film, we see how the son of a Nazi Commander became, by default, a victim of the gassing of the Jews in concentration camps because of his friendship with a Jewish child at the time.

As we know, children have no prejudices except they have been taught. Unknown to the commander, his son would become a victim of his heartless orders to gas the Jews in one of the concentration camps. Although this film is based on fiction, it does indeed show how social connectedness could lead to events that we, as individuals, have no control over, especially with the growing young generation beginning to see the truth and working in unity, friendship & solidarity.

We are all indeed connected...

Let us care enough to connect

Connect to the plight of the disadvantaged people, BAME

There is room for all in our Society

Let us be bold & courageous & stand up for equality

Stand up for justice and fair play in all nations

#There is unity in Diversity#

#There is power in Diversity#

#There is growth in Diversity#

#Black lives matter#

#We know all lives matter#

#Help is needed with black lives matter so that black lives can matter too#

#Rise up above colour#

#Rise up and show love#

#Rise up for justice & equality#

It is the right thing to do. Now is the time…

To George Floyd and others killed unjustly on account of the colour of their skin… (Rest in peace).

Equality and Diversity in Social Work & Social Care

What is Equality?

"Equality is the right of different groups of people to have a similar social position and receive the same treatment" - Cambridge English Dictionary

"Equality is the right of different groups of people to receive the same treatment" – American Dictionary

Equality is underpinned by a legal framework that places statutory duties on individuals, communities, and organisations to ensure that no one under the protected characteristics is disadvantaged.

Equality Act 2010 protected characteristics include the multi-dimensional layers of diversity, including age, disability, gender, race, religion or belief, marriage, etc.

In simplistic terms, equality means that all individuals should be treated equally and have an equal chance to experience day-to-day life, work, and opportunities equally as others regardless of any of the characteristics mentioned above. In other words, equality ensures that diversity is acknowledged and respected.

Organisations, Local Authorities, the Government at all levels have a moral duty to consider the Equality Act 2010, protected characteristics and ensure that every person can fulfil their potentials at work regardless of these characteristics.

"Every person, regardless of their ethnicity or background, should be able to fulfil their potentials at work. That is the business case as well as the moral case" (Macgregor Smith Review 2017).

What is Diversity?

Diversity - "The fact of many different types of things or people being included in something; a range of different things or people" - Cambridge Dictionary

"The condition or fact of being different or varied; variety" – American Dictionary

Diversity means the difference in people, behaviour, culture, language, religion, beliefs, etc. Diversity forms one of the nine Professional Capabilities Framework (PCF) domains initially created by the Social Work Reform Board, now adopted by the British Association of Social Workers (BASW) in 2018. The framework designed to help Social workers practice more efficiently highlights diversity as the third domain. The terminology Diversity & Equality are often used together.

Diversity: Social Workers must recognise diversity and apply anti-discriminatory and anti-oppressive principles in practice *(TCSW, 2012; BASW 2018).*

Social Work England Professional Standards (1) stipulates: ***"SWs must promote the rights, strengths, and wellbeing of people, families, and communities. They should recognise differences across diverse communities and challenge the impact of disadvantage and discrimination on people and their families and communities. Promote social justice, helping to confront and resolve issues of inequality and inclusion".***

BASW PCF domain 3 (Diversity) states; Social Workers should:

Recognise and apply anti-discriminatory and anti-oppressive principles in practice:

- *Recognise the complexity of identity and diversity of experience and apply this to practice.*
- *Recognise discriminatory practices and develop a range of approaches to appropriately challenge service users, colleagues, and senior staff.*

- *Critically reflect on and manage the power of your role in your relationship with others.*

"In a multicultural society, social workers are expected to recognise diversity in their practice and actively tackle oppression" Vern Pitt 2011.

What is Cultural Competence in Social Work?

Cultural competence in social work "entails understanding the cultural differences of people in need of social services. Social workers who demonstrate cultural competence strive to understand the cultures of the people they serve and approach them with cultural sensitivity and respect" (Virginia Commonwealth University).

Cultural competence is simply a professional's ability to appreciate and interact effectively with people from various cultural backgrounds. One of the best ways to grow in this area is to learn about other cultures.

Professionals don't necessarily have to be experts, but it would help if they had a keenness to acquire new knowledge and a willingness to practice. For a Social Worker working, for example, in Children's services, a child and a young person's cultural heritage and identity cannot be overlooked. It should be at the forefront of practice. Cultural sensitivity is demanded in social care, social work, and public service. The need for cultural responsiveness has become amplified and widely advocated in the wake of the murder of George Floyd. More awareness and attention have been created to racial inequality in our Society in the months following the event.

Social Workers, Foster carers, and Government officials/politicians should pay more attention and discuss cultural competence. Ignorance should no longer be an excuse. In late 2020, in the news and social media, a prominent public member, FA Chairman Gregg Clarke, was forced to resign from his position after referring to black footballers as coloured. He used outdated and inappropriate terminology whilst addressing British MPs in Parliament. Unfortunately for him, he paid the price for the improper use of language, especially in the tense racial climate of the very extraordinary and noteworthy year of 2020.

It is important to stress that many more will fall victims. It seemed like basic knowledge around appropriate terminology is not common within the football association even though it is richly endowed with players from diverse backgrounds. This incident highlights that education is needed at all levels. During the heat of George Floyd's protests, Labour MP in the UK Diane Abbott proposed that members of the Parliament consider the prospect of undertaking training in unconscious bias. Labour leader Keir Starmer favoured such learning activity for the Labour Party members and stated that he would undertake the same. It is optimistic that leaders and influential members of our Society are beginning to hold some dialogue on education and change in this area. It will be great to see more meaningful and practical actions.

In Social Work, the importance of cultural competence cannot be over-emphasized both in Children's Services and Adult Services. Recent years have seen the influx of children into care from various cultural backgrounds with parents from different cultures. Social workers must promote all vulnerable children's identity, which is crucial for building their self-esteem.

A Community Care UK article in late 2020 by Tina Amongi titled *"Food is a marker of identity: Supporting foster children's cultural heritage"* gives an excellent insight to social workers and caregivers. It stresses the need to pay serious attention to Looked after children's cultural identity needs to avoid "cultural dislocation".

One of the core values of Social work is the pursuit of social justice, anti-oppressive and anti-discriminatory practice. Social workers cannot claim to effectively embed this principle without acknowledging and respecting diversity, promoting inclusion and integration in Society. Most of the service users we work with in social care, particularly children and young people, come in diverse forms, with different cultures, experiences, world views, etc. Social work is a career like no other, a purely humanitarian service to Society's most vulnerable. If social workers cannot genuinely work with diversity, it is impossible to make the very difference that the career purports to create. At the very least, the role requires cultural competence. Social workers and social care workers may wonder what this looks like in the most practical terms. Well, let's look at this straightforward and easy-to-understand concept - The VOT Diversity Acrostic Poem.

In the UK, in recent years, we have seen a higher influx of children and young people into care from various cultural backgrounds. Social workers must promote all vulnerable children's identity, which is crucial in building their self-esteem.

WORKING WITH DIVERSITY & DEVELOPING CULTURALLY SENSITIV PRACTICE IN SOCIAL WORK AND SOCIAL CARE

DECIDE TO BE A CULTURALLY SENSITIVE PRACTITIONE

INVITE PEOPLE TO TALK ABOUT THEIR CULTURES, VALUES, BELIEFS AND EXPERIENCES

VALUE THEIR HISTORY, INDIVIDUALITY AND DIFFERENCES

EXPLORE CLIENTS REALITIES, SHOW CURIOSITY

REFLECT UPON INFORMATION & KNOWLEDGE RECEIVED

SCRUTINIZE YOURSELF - PERSONAL SWOT ANALYS (STRENGTHS, WEAKNESSES, OPPORTUNITIES & THREATS)

IDENTIFY STRATEGIES TO AID YOUR WORK

TRAIN YOURSELF TO TREAT PEOPLE & FAMILIES INDIVIDUALLY

YIELD TO CULTURALLY SENSITIVE PRACTICE

Diversity Acrostic Poem

Working with Diversity & Developing Culturally Sensitive Practice in Social Work and Social Care

D - Decide to be a Culturally Sensitive Practitioner

I - Invite People to talk about their cultures, values, beliefs, and experiences

V - Value their history, individuality, and differences

E - Explore client's realities, show curiosity

R - Reflect upon information and knowledge received

S - Scrutinise yourself – personal SWOT analysis (Strengths, Weaknesses, Opportunities & Threats)

I - Identify strategies to aid your work

T - Train yourself to treat people, children, and families individually

Y - Yield to culturally sensitive practice

D
DECIDE

DIVERSITY

D – Decide to be a Culturally Sensitive Practitioner

Decide to be a culturally sensitive practitioner. As previously mentioned, Diversity forms one of the nine Professional Capabilities Framework (PCF) domains created by the Social Work Reform Board in 2012 to help Social Workers practice efficiently. The framework was adopted by the British Association of Social Work (BASW) in 2018. Diversity is the third Professional Capability Domain, and it states:

"Social Workers must recognise diversity and apply anti-discriminatory and anti-oppressive principles in practice" (TCSW 2012, BASW 2018)".

BASW Code of Ethics for Social Work (Social Justice) states that: *Social workers have a responsibility to promote social justice in Society and with the people with whom they work. They must acknowledge diversity & challenge discrimination.*

Working effectively with diversity and becoming a culturally competent practitioner is a fundamental requirement in the social worker's career, and it is key to becoming a proficient social worker. You must decide the kind of social worker you wish to be, a proficient one or a non-proficient one. This little detail is worth reflecting on at this stage. It may require you to consider the reasons why you came into the humanitarian field of social work. Is it to be more available to a particular group of people than the others? Or is it to make a real difference in Society to those who need it the most? It may be that you accidentally came into the field or that you were looking for a lucrative career with job prospects. Social workers remain very well sought after. Perhaps you chose the profession for other reasons and hadn't fully considered what the career entailed and what would be required of you in the field. However, it needs to be stressed that social work is a dynamic field where professional accountability and cultural competence is required. *You, therefore, need to decide to be a culturally sensitive practitioner.*

Working effectively with diversity and becoming a culturally competent practitioner is a fundamental requirement in a Social Worker's career, and it is the key to becoming a skilled Social Worker.

I

INVITE

DIVERSITY

I – Invite people to talk about their cultures, values, beliefs, and experiences

Invite people to talk about their cultures, values, beliefs, and experiences. To learn about a person or a group of people, you must be prepared to listen and hear. You must be willing and prepared to engage with them actively. Curiosity is vital in social work practice. You need to be curious about others, where they have come from, the things they hold dear, their lived experiences that have shaped them through life. Social work practitioners must not depend solely on a certain group of people's stories or experiences to understand or rationalise other people's behaviours. Everyone has their own stories, even within the same perceived culture groups. Professionals need to come away from the "one size fits all approach" or using "one tape to measure all".

At the risk of stating the obvious, carrying out social work interventions or caring for the vulnerable requires the act of individualising. It is a well-known rationale stipulated in the NHS England Constitution, and it needs to remain at the forefront of practice.

The agelong saying, "Knowledge is Power", still applies and remains relevant. Information is needed in whichever field of service you find yourself in—social care, health care, adult or children services, public services, etc. You should allow service users to educate you on how to relate to and work with them. You can learn so much from service users by hearing their stories, which helps formulate interventions. Let service users tell you their individual stories.

Let me tell you the story of my life.

Relying on X or Y to tell you the story of Z or the actions of a person/group to dictate the story of others is a dangerous and unethical practice in the humanitarian field of social work—an area you elected to come into to make a change. Presumably, most people who choose to come into the field or career of social work are people seeking to make a positive change.

When we invite people or service users to speak to us about their experiences, it is crucial to engage in an open and non-judgemental manner. This allows us to listen to, hear, and understand the stories of others and intervene effectively in their lives. A professional can listen from a position of acceptance and empathy to hear what is said to them and empathise. They listen not just for the fun of listening, but they seize the opportunity to acquire knowledge and skills in wide-ranging areas. They can also learn to challenge issues around cultural diversity constructively.

As a social work student, I came across the Motivational Interviewing (MI) Techniques of Miller & Rollnick (2002) and invariably fell in love with it due to its simplicity. The model was posited for intervention with service users affected by drug and alcohol misuse. It provides vital elements for successful interaction that influence positive change. The advocated concept of "reflective listening" is helpful in this discourse. It is one of the essential skills required when you invite people to talk to you about themselves and their experiences. There is intrinsic value in being curious and learning about other cultures. It enriches your knowledge and broadens your perspective. Your expertise becomes versatile.

There is a huge misconception around classifying people of colour together, e.g. Black people, Asian people, Latinos, etc. These people's cultures can vary significantly regardless of whether they share the same colour tone, have the same look, same type of hair, same accent, etc. For example, black people in the United States, the United Kingdom, the Caribbean Islands, and Africa vary widely regardless of having the same skin colour. It is essential to learn about an individual's unique self. The best way is to *invite people to talk about their own cultures, values, beliefs, and experiences.*

> ***"When you talk, you are only repeating what you already know, but if you listen, you may learn something new."***
>
> *-Dalai Lama*

Relying on X or Y to tell you the story of Z or the actions of a person/group to dictate the story of others is a dangerous and unethical practice in the humanitarian field of Social work.

VALUE

DIVERSITY

V – Value Service users' history, individuality, and differences

It is one thing to acquire information and enhance your knowledge; however, using such is the key to building cultural competence. Social workers obtain and have custody of service user's stories which they manage on a day to day basis. Service users become vulnerable to you by sharing their stories, those things they hold dear, the experiences that have shaped them etc. Social work and social care professionals need to value and respect their account. These experiences may or may not be familiar to you or may differ from your own experiences in immense depths. Valuing and respecting other people's experiences are the keywords here. Social Workers must not minimise, reduce, or undermine those values and experiences or the difference.

Professionals do not have to like or go along with the perspective they are presented with. They only need to acknowledge, try to understand, and make sense of those experiences that have shaped their service user's lives. The essential skill required here for social work professionals is to remain curious and open-minded.

As a black social work professional, I have observed some white colleagues keep interaction to the bare minimum or choose not to interact with colleagues from black ethnic minority groups. I sometimes struggle to understand how such practitioners can carry out successful, robust interventions with vulnerable children and young people from these cultural backgrounds. Maintaining such a position will impede any reasonable or meaningful social work intervention to vulnerable service users.

Undermining people's cultures, beliefs, and experiences diminishes them psychologically and can lower their self-esteem, impacting their emotional, mental health. This is not the aim of social work. Social care and social work staff invariably need to connect with people in small ways to make significant positive change. *They should value the service user's history, individuality, and differences.*

Undermining people's cultures, beliefs, and experiences diminishes them psychologically and can lower their self-esteem, impacting their emotional, mental health.

E
EXPLORE

DIVERSITY

E - Explore client's realities, show curiosity

Explore client's realities and show curiosity. Having gathered as much information about others, including your service users. You need to weigh up, reason out and actively evaluate the information you have received. Remember, this is your service user's lived experiences, and for some, it is a stark bitter reality. Some service users, particularly vulnerable children, have passed through an awful lot in their often very young life. They have lived through more in their lives than the professionals intervening with them. They usually have suffered severe childhood trauma, abuse, severe neglect, loss of childhood, etc. It is not an age factor for some of these children but an experience factor. Once brought into care, they further suffer the trauma of loss and separation from their loved ones and close family whom they have known and cherished in their lives.

Social workers and foster carers must remember that regardless of whatever abuse service users, particularly children and young people, have suffered before coming into care, they still have a deep-rooted bond with their families. Emotions they may never share with the professionals working with them. Regardless of the dire circumstances that may have led children into the system, they naturally still love their families, mums, dads, siblings, etc., in ways that professionals may never quantify. This little detail is sometimes overlooked by those working with them. Some vulnerable children's experiences may be unique and not familiar or sometimes not understood by professionals of other cultures working with them. This is okay; we are all learners. Social workers are very busy professionals, so it is often a challenge to deeply explore service users' culture and experiences to connect better. They should, however, attempt or show intent. At this stage, a social worker's ability to show empathy is put to the test—an ability to put yourself in other people's shoes and feel their pain. As a professional, the question should be: Can you relate to those sad, deep, and sometimes heart-wrenching life stories of your vulnerable service users from different cultural backgrounds? If so, how so? Empathy remains central to social work and social care.

Dan Hughes, Psychologist and Dyadic Developmental Psychotherapy founder, advocates a deep connection to service users' plight to create positive behaviour change. Social work professionals should show an active interest in people's lived experiences, culture, and beliefs, seek to understand their vulnerabilities, and offer a genuine desire to support them in overcoming their challenges. This is called having a caring attitude. Social work is indeed a caring profession. A career in Social care is a career in caring for and supporting vulnerable individuals, children, and families.

Undertaking some research into how best to support service users is very vital. The study should start with the service users themselves. For example, in children's services, professionals must refer to the child's voice (Children Act 1989), particularly children from black and other minority ethnic backgrounds whose voices often get lost. This advice may sound ordinary and mundane; however, it is not. Admittedly, one of the significant challenges facing social service today is the very loss of the children or vulnerable young people's voices in interventions that affect them. This is more so for children from other ethnic backgrounds where professionals are not familiar with or lack cultural knowledge.

Sometimes these children's voices are lost, and so are their identities. It is only whilst knowing about those things that mean much to the vulnerable children that professionals can achieve great success with their interventions. Preserving children's identity is key to building their self-esteem, helping them to thrive and achieve despite it all. Social workers should strive to explore service users' realities with professional curiosity.

Social workers need to carry out deep exploration of service user's experiences. At this stage, a social worker's ability to demonstrate empathy is put to the test—the ability to put yourself in other people's shoes and to feel their pain.

R

REFLECT

DIVERSITY

R – Reflect upon information and ideas received

This dimension is about reflecting upon information and ideas received from service users. Casting your mind back to question and evaluate your performance is often referred to as critical reflection in social work. It forms one of the Social Work Professionals Capabilities Framework (PCF) Domains. Reflecting regularly on events and performance helps to enhance your intervention skills as a professional. It increases a professional's ability to analyse situations and make judgements around complex day-to-day work undertaken with service users Schon (1983). Critical reflection is a reasoning process, an actual act of thinking, probing yourself to analyse events. You regularly question your interventions, your response to issues and circumstances, explore your feelings and ways you can do things better next time. E.g. "What am I proud of today? What can I do better next time? What do I need to change in my way of working?

Dan Siegel (2010), in his work "Mindsight", Interpersonal Neurobiology talks about the human reflective ability to perceive the mind of self and others & feel empathy for others. The mind's power to change the brain's functioning, focusing on the internal World to modify "*Diving into the sea within ourselves*". You essentially undergo a deep self-probing and reasoning process. Critical reflection is essential for working with diversity because it can help you connect with your thought process, including your psychosocial development, to make sense of things as a social work professional. It enables you to challenge yourself and your thinking to find new ways of working. As a professional, you can connect to those values, biases, and prejudices, including those stories you were told growing up. And how they have shaped and continue to shape your perspective in your personal and professional life. Reflection allows professionals to be self-aware and to remain balanced and objective in their interventions. Professionals ensure that they do not let their judgments or preconceived notions to be a huge influencing factor. Social work and social care professionals should not hesitate to challenge themselves and others as part of their work-life, even though this can be a painful exercise.

In their work on critical reflection, Brown, and Rutter (2008) suggest that critical thinking can sometimes be challenging, threatening, and anxiety-provoking, leading to unpleasant consequences or responses from other people. Social work staff should recognise their core feelings and seek help to address any events impacting negatively on their emotional wellbeing. They should use management, mentor, or peer supervision to support themselves.

At the critical reflection stage, a professional can form a new world view after processing and making sense of the information handed to them by their service users or those they encounter regularly. Looking back at your performance to essentially debrief yourself helps make your practice and interventions better, which could be around anti-oppression and anti-discrimination. When people or service users choose to lay their lived experiences and feelings bare at your feet, there are usually deep feelings associated. The service users are often in search of help, understanding, affirmation, etc. A social worker's role is to give that help and support.

Social Work Author Neil Thompson advocates the need for social work professionals to develop the act of “reflecting in action” and “reflecting on action” so that the outcome of reflection benefits service users promptly during the intervention and not just retrospectively. This concept is also very relevant in this discourse area. It simply means the ability to reflect, think on your feet and act promptly, which could be around issues of oppression and discrimination.

In the Autumn of 2020, Britain’s popular Dance Band Diversity showcased a powerful performance on Britain’s got Talent (BGT) show described as the summary of the things that affected society in 2020. The performance reflected on Black Lives Matter along with the Coronavirus Pandemic and more. Rightly so because BLM was indeed one of the significant events in the very noteworthy year. It would be impossible for history to ignore this. Interestingly, Ofcom, UK received about 25,000 viewer complaints about the performance which were dismissed. The rationale for the complaints was that BGT was not the “right stage” for highlighting this. I agree with Ashley Banjo when he responded, "What is the right stage?”.

"Why can we talk about a multitude of other issues" on the BGT stage but not racism? The performance was a creative piece of dance art that highlighted racism and black lives matter amongst other significant events of the notable year. The whole presentation was deeply reflective and should be applauded.

"I feel proud that we [Diversity] have become a bit of a symbol for something that I want to live up to. I want to be able to speak up — and not just about racism". – Ashley Banjo, Diversity

S
NOTES
TO
SELF
SCRUTINIZ

DIVERSITY

S – Scrutinise yourself - Personal SWOT Analysis (Strengths, Weaknesses, Opportunity, Threats)

Scrutinise yourself – personal SWOT Analysis of a professional's (strengths, weaknesses, opportunity, threats) follows from the previous letter (R) reflection. Scrutinising yourself means doing a deep, honest examination of yourself to understand your personality, capabilities, limitations and learning needs. It means taking account of your perspective on life, values & beliefs concerning diversity or cultural diversity & how they might affect your practice—examining stereotypes, prejudices, assumptions, your attitude, words, and actions, etc. Professionals must probe their prejudices, & biases, etc., both conscious and unconscious. It is important to note here that most biases are implicit, which remains unhelpful in practice. In this section, it is worth noting that every individual, regardless of race, culture, etc., has their prejudices and beliefs that they were either born into or passed down from family, otherwise handed by the Society.

Here is a short story very close to home.

My father's perspective: (May his soul rest in peace): Once upon a time, my father was on my case to get married soon as I was perceived to be at that age of marriage. And why not? I had finished my University degree, and I had, in fact, concluded my Masters' degree, so nothing was stopping me from getting married. It was the next logical step, especially from the typical African (Nigerian) family perspective. A promising young daughter, having concluded her University education, is expected to get married to a responsible young man from a decent family, have children, and live happily ever after! At this stage, my conversations with my dad, usually over the phone due to living far apart, even a continent away, included subtle reminders to find a husband! The conversations always carried silent undertones that simply said: "Have you got news for me?". In other words, "When will you be bringing home a suitor/fiancé to introduce to us?". I also had the pleasure of hearing about other mates of mine from our hometown who had recently got married straight after University! As the months and years passed by, these subtle conversations became more desperate. I was the first daughter of six children, which was of considerable significance.

He was looking forward to having that proud Daddy moment like most fathers. The message was clear; it is time to get married! So, you can imagine the excitement I felt when I met someone, and I looked forward to telling my dad that I would make him proud! I rang up and said, "Dad, I am getting married!" He was undoubtedly very pleased and immediately proceeded to ask where my fiancé was from, a typical question asked by the average Nigerian parent. I stated that he was from Spain.

My dad responded: "Oh great, he lives in Spain, where is he from? What village is he from? Where are his parents from?". My dad, of course, presumed that my fiancé was no doubt going to be a Nigerian; hence he wanted to know what village or town my fiancé was from? Nigeria has four major geographical regions, Northern, Southern, Eastern & Western. I am from the Eastern part of the country. Parents would usually prefer their children to marry someone from the same geographical region for proximity purposes and cultural similarities. The thought process is that their children would remain as close as possible to home and the things familiar to them after marriage. In Nigeria, a person is from the settlement where their parents, grandparents, great grandparents came from going back generations.

They are not actually from where they were born, as it is in the Western World, unless they were born in their family lineage location or settlement. This was precisely why my dad asked where my fiancé and his parents were from? I continued to answer that they were all from Spain and then dropped the "shock". He is white from Spain; both his parents are white from Spain too"! The penny dropped, and it took my dad a few minutes to digest that information. You could most certainly hear the loud inaudible silence down the telephone line. He immediately came back to me saying: "Oh no, there is no need to rush; marriage is not what you rush into; you need to take your time"….

My dad's response was a fascinating one from someone who had been advocating strongly for me to get married! He was now taking a back step because I presented someone out of the norm. Someone who is not only from a different geographical region in Nigeria, but indeed from another world in my dad's *eyes! "Oyibo" (a white man). My dad was now advocating for me to slow down. He felt that I had settled for a white man because I was under pressure and unable to secure myself a black Nigerian man. He then said that he did not think it was a good idea for me to marry a man who was not the same as me, who did not understand our culture and was most certainly going to draw me further away from my family. My dad was a well-read and educated man, a Civil Engineer who obtained his Ph.D./Doctorate at age 67, although sadly, he died two years after. He, however, fulfilled his lifelong academic ambition as a person who valued education. I feel that my dad although quite literate operated under the scope of his knowledge and his lack of familiarity around interracial marriage or "white culture". I was sure that my dad meant no harm by his advice; he had not met my fiancé at this time. He was simply sticking to what he knew, his familiar territory. I would like to posit that his perspective was formed by his feeling of uncertainty, lack of knowledge, and preconceived notions. As an individual, he needed more education in this unknown area. I am pleased to say that he did open himself to learn and when he eventually met my husband, he embraced him, and they got on very well. As a matter of fact, in my dad's typical upfront and blunt manner, he stated when they met that I was lucky to find myself such a handsome husband!*

***

This story's learning is that we've all got something due to cultural differences, traditions, family stories told to us, preconceived notions etc. They may only surface when faced with a particular scenario or event/s. No individual can shy away from this. We first and foremost need to recognise them and be open to learning to have a good shot at changing those views.

Before coming into the Social work humanitarian field, I studied business administration and worked in business banking for a short while. In business, you often talk about SWOT Analysis which is an evaluation of business "temperature", etc., to plan and develop effective business strategies. Companies look at the four core areas: strengths, weaknesses, opportunities, and threats. They compare the internal factors (strengths & weaknesses) against external factors (opportunities and threats) to strategically position themselves for growth and development. The SWOT Analysis has been personalised in social work and other practice areas in recent times. The idea is that professionals can carry out a personal SWOT analysis of themselves and effectively do the same examination that organisations do.

This will enable them to understand their strengths and weaknesses, the threats to their growth and development including opportunities available to them. As a professional, you consider your perspective, values, beliefs and understanding around diversity & how they might affect your practice. As mentioned in the previous section, we need to deliberate on the stories from our parents, grandparents, and family lineage. Those stories we were told in our childhood that have stayed with us over time. And how they have shaped and continue to shape our lives. Everyone has something. Dr Robin DiAngelo – A Professor of Education at the University of California, a US expert in anti-racism & anti-bias, has continued to advocate for a deep understanding of self in tackling bias. She is the author of the International Bestseller - *White Fragility -Why it's so hard for white people to talk about racism* published in 2018. Dr DiAngelo posits that white people are essentially born into and bred in a system of inequality through no making of theirs. An inculcated and internalised notion of superiority that white people cannot miss—A fundamental white privilege that sprang from white supremacy.

The idea of inferiority is needed to maintain superiority leading to racism (conscious or unconscious). She further posits that anti-black is profoundly ingrained in the white culture, the notion that black people are inferior. The average four-year-old child soon learns that it is better to be white than black… That the system we live in portrays no inherent value in people of colour's perspective or experiences. According to DiAngelo, white people are not often taught the loss of living in racial segregation, and some can move from "cradle to grave in segregation". Some indeed choose to do so. She surmises that people of colour distrust in schools & institutions are rational, including black people's default view of white people as racists. This is due to decades of slavery, negative racial experiences, long history of distrust, etc. Unfortunately, this default view sadly paints all white people with the same brush, which is not the case. She refers to Society default to the reproduction of racism as a system failure that has continued for many generations. As a social work professional, I must admit that I continue to find Dr DiAngelo's arguments very insightful and fascinating. It provides a good awareness of the fragility of white colleagues.

It also helps to form a perspective on this age-long problem of racism. Admittedly, it is only in understanding the root of a problem that any effective solution could be proffered to this obvious social problem. It means that for professionals to reflect a truthful narrative of themselves, they need to consider their psychosocial development to identify any learned behaviour that needs to change and how to do so.

By scrutinising yourself, you can identify your strengths and consolidate them to mitigate your weaknesses around diversity. And this will help form a positive world view on race and equality. You can also assess your learning needs and pursue training opportunities to enhance your weaknesses. Following the worldwide protests over George Floyd's death and the turbulent racial climate in 2020, suggestions were made for British MPs to undertake mandatory training on unconscious bias. The suggestion was immediately met with resistance by several Conservative MPs. The opposition was criticised by Labour MP Diane Abbott, who stated in Aug 2020: *"Nothing says bias like someone who absolutely refuses to discuss the possibility that they might be unconscious bias."*

The resistance seemed like a missed opportunity for MPs who are effectively public servants dealing with a society of diverse people. Self-scrutiny around diversity will help professionals and politicians individually identify their weaknesses and seek learning to close any perceived gaps.

As a Social Work professional, you should be able to challenge those deeply entrenched prejudices, stereotypes, generational "hand me downs" from your family. And consider how they have shaped and continue to shape your perspective in your personal and professional life.

Acknowledging white privilege, the possibility of conscious or unconscious bias is fundamental in engaging with diversity and promoting justice and equality.

Regardless of race, culture, etc., every individual has their individual beliefs, prejudices & biases that they are either born into or are passed down from family generations otherwise handed by Society at large.

"Racism hurts people of colour 24/7, interrupting it is more important than my feelings, ego or self – image" – Dr Robin DiAngelo

IDENTIFY

DIVERSITY

I – Identify Strategies to aid your Work.

Identify strategies to aid your work. Within this section, professionals should begin to ask themselves the following questions:

- ✓ *How do I, as a professional, rewrite history and change my racial construct to embrace diversity?*
- ✓ *As a social work or social care professional, how do I engage with authenticity and reality?*
- ✓ *How can I develop an empathic disposition to people of difference, disadvantaged people, and the less privileged?*
- ✓ *How do I ensure that my personal views assimilated over time do not obstruct my work with clients different from me?*
- ✓ *How do I acknowledge, respect, and engage with diversity?*

Social work and social care professionals continue to have a duty to promote anti-discriminatory and anti-oppressive practice; agreeably, it is one of the core principles in this field. Professionals must identify and access training, research, management & mentor supervision and make good meaning of the same in this area of practice. One of the core requirements for a social work practitioner is to constantly engage in Continued Professional Development (CPD) to improve practice. Professionals can use available models of practice in supporting vulnerable children and families, and adults from diverse backgrounds. They can also use models such as the Signs of Safety (SOS) to look at what is working well in practice, particularly in interacting and solving problems for children and families from different backgrounds. The Secure Base caregiving attachment model used by some Local Authorities in the UK gives a simple model for considering vulnerable children's needs and meeting those needs. Dimensions 3 (Acceptance -Building the child's self-esteem) and dimension 4 (Co-operation – Helping the child feel effective) can help promote anti-oppressive and anti-discriminatory caregiving for looked after children.

The "Social Graces" illustrative tool developed by John Burnham, Alison Roper-Hall, and colleagues (1992) to address social inequality presented an extended version of the equality Act 2010 protected characteristics. It is a helpful reminder of those diversity characteristics that form an individual's identity, which may not necessarily be exhaustive, especially with new emerging orientations. A BASW article by Rebekah Pierre in July 2020 is also a good reminder of the Social Graces' model. The idea of naming the power differentials helps professionals identify and address their biases and preconceptions. Most professionals will have areas within the Equality act protected characteristics and "Social Graces", which poses a challenge and impacts on their ability to work in a culturally competent manner.

Practitioners should research and explore widely to identify strategies that can aid them in this area and line of work. Social care and social work professionals must develop and nurture a learning attitude. The famous saying: "Life is a learning curve", remains relevant. Continuous learning is required to ensure that vulnerable service users' best interest is achieved.

Practical strategies could be liaising with and obtaining information and support from your colleagues from other backgrounds to inform your work. This will mitigate situations where professionals are worried about approaching issues or getting things wrong.

It is often the norm to underestimate black colleagues' education, knowledge, and skills, particularly when they did not study in the big nations in the Western World, such as the UK, US, Canada, etc. Regardless of where they are from, be it black or white, each individual or professional has unique talents that should be given a fair opportunity to soar. Equality in the workplace is about promoting all professionals, regardless of their cultural background, to grow progressively alongside each other. Most workplaces lack anti-racism policies or strategies that actively promote equality and diversity. Organisations should be deliberate and show active interest and commitment to tackling inequality and racism. They can ask for help and support from BAME staff within their establishment.

The Equality Act 2010 provides a direction of travel for anti-discriminatory practice; however, the desired outcomes can only be achieved when the leaders intentionally create and implement suitable strategies. There have been calls for racism to be tackled or treated separately from the other protected characteristics. The notion is that although there is no hierarchy in inequality, combating racism requires prioritising due to the deeply rooted nature of it spanning over decades.

Useful strategies could be liaising and obtaining information and support from colleagues of diverse backgrounds.

T

TRAIN

DIVERSITY

T - Train yourself to treat people and families individually

Train yourself to treat people and families individually. This dimension follows from identifying strategies to aid your work. Having gone through all the steps enumerated above, you must identify strategies to help you to put acquired skills and knowledge to practice. It means developing the act of treating individuals, families, and service users, including those from other backgrounds, individually, not collectively. I.e. Professionals departing from the approach of using "one measuring tape to measure all" and stepping into individualised one – to – one intervention with service users. This prevents social workers from falling into the trap of generalising or succumbing to common statements such as:

"X Y Z children are usually feral."

"X Y Z children are aggressive and violent."

"Black children don't fit in."

"Black children need to be placed with black carers."

"Unaccompanied asylum seekers are dangerous"...

Statements like these do little to enhance the plight of vulnerable children. They instead stigmatise the already disadvantaged children before they've even had a chance to speak up or defend themselves.

Working with diversity and becoming a culturally sensitive practitioner means that a professional is in tune with the fact that the vulnerable service users they work with may come from different backgrounds, diverse situations, and circumstances. They all need equal help and support.

Every person has their personality, history, culture, and world view that has shaped them over time into the person they have become today. Likewise, for children in care, their home life or general life experience before coming into the care system shapes them into the individuals observed by the professionals who work with them. It is essential to remind ourselves that those children were not necessarily born that way. However, with high warmth and high nurture from their carers, they can thrive again. It means that professionals can still make a significant positive difference and influence the direction of children from all backgrounds. Children can be supported to break out from negative behaviour patterns and pursue the route to enjoying and achieving. It is in connecting deeply with individual circumstances that professionals can carry out robust interventions that create change.

"You must connect in order to correct" (Dan Hughes).

Professionals must seek a clear & reasonable understanding of children and families, service users' culture & circumstances to be able to tailor their work to meet those needs. Social workers, particularly in children's services, should train themselves to explore vulnerable children and young people's identity and culture. It enables them to put together a detailed life story from the very onset of their work and, most importantly, share these valuables with fellow professionals and carers. A well-compiled life story essentially helps professionals to work well together to support children's identity, which is fundamental in realising positive outcomes for vulnerable children. Social care and social work professionals need to be proactive in identifying available resources and cultural competence materials. A Community Care article by Tina Amongi, in October 2020, *"Food is a marker of Identity": supporting the cultural heritage of children looked after"*, is a brilliant article that gives a good insight in a snapshot. It highlights how social workers and foster carers should pay serious attention to children's cultural identity to avoid "cultural dislocation".

There was a considerable emphasis on social worker's critical role in ensuring that Looked after children maintain their identity and remain in touch with their heritage. Social workers should strive to obtain and collate adequate information for the looked after children and prospective carers to enable their cultural needs to be adequately met. Social workers remain accountable and should display appropriate skills to safeguard vulnerable children and adults, including preserving their cultures. It means that social workers must recognise the multi-dimensional layers of diversity, including the protected characteristics such as race, disability, class, economic status, age, gender, faith, etc. They should bear in mind that a person's life experience may include oppression and marginalisation while another person's experience may be of privilege and power, etc. And this shapes a person's identity and general outlook on life. It is indeed a mandatory requirement for social workers to be proficient in cultural competence at the very minimum - developing the ability to treat people from all backgrounds individually, fairly, and equitably. They learn to balance power to impact service users positively in real-time.

Social work professionals, particularly in children's services, should train themselves to explore the identity and culture of vulnerable children and young people to put together a detailed life story.

Having done all there is to stand; you must stand firm and be a Culturally Competent Practitioner.

Y
YIELD

DIVERSITY

Y – Yield to Culturally Sensitive Practice

Yielding to culturally sensitive practice is the final domain of the VOT Diversity Acrostic Poem. As a social work professional who made an intentional decision to enter the humanitarian field of social work to help the vulnerable, you must yield to culturally sensitive practice. It forms the basis of Social work practice. You cannot claim to put a child in the centre and work in their best interest if you consciously or unconsciously ignore or minimise their cultures or the cultures of those like them. Your practice could effectively be described as superficial and just scraping through the surface.

Having finally navigated through the Diversity Acrostic Poem, the individual letters, the associated phrases, you must form a view on diversity. As social care and social work professionals, having done all there is to stand, you must stand firm and become a Culture Competent Practitioner.

You must understand culture as dynamic, challenge stereotypes, reject prescribed cultural understanding in favour of focusing on individual circumstances to provide positive interventions. You must own your practice and train others. In so doing, you become a Professional Leader in your field - BASW Professional Capabilities Domain (PCF) nine.

"Lack of knowledge or understanding of a particular client's culture, family dynamics, or world view often gives rise to resistance and could delay or harm the social work intervention process"- **(Comas-Diaz & Jacobson 1991).**

As Social Workers, we must seek to recognise and have a reasonable understanding of the service users' world view to translate presented behaviours and proffer enduring solutions.

Every child matters

Every person matters

All lives matter

Let black lives matter too

Diversity is the norm in nature. Being part of a minority is being part of the whole.

How can black people collaborate in promoting anti-racist practice?

It is often very costly for black people to challenge racism; hence they need their white colleagues to support them. Challenging racism in the workplace can frequently label black people as "troublesome", "difficult", "the victim", etc. It can also lead to stigmatisation, stagnancy in the workplace, and job loss. Regardless, black people must continue to raise awareness and challenge racism when it occurs because not doing so contributes to racial discrimination.

Some black people choose not to speak about racism because they are under the misapprehension that discrimination will not be directed at them. This group feel that they are somewhat "special" or "superior" to the other black people or people subjected to racism. The notion is that they are more accepted for whatever reasons. Those reasons could be that they have a lighter skin colour, are of mixed race, are born and educated in the Western World, or have the white American or British accent. The list goes on... Black people should show a unified front towards a common goal and avoid division.

The other group of black professionals separate themselves from fellow black colleagues to fit into the white majority group. This could be to situate themselves in their quest for belonging, to access better work roles or ascend to higher job positions, among other reasons. I believe that racism thrives excellently because black people do not come together in one voice and stand firmly against it. Black people are not as unified as they could be. This little minute detail is not missed in Society, and it remains a recipe for continued racial discrimination. In the workplace, we can be seen competing against each other to prove ourselves and secure our positions.

Some black people are under the illusion or false security that they fit in better, while others feel that they are liked better, are more established, hence untouchable. Black people and other minority ethnic groups need to unite and look out for each other because we are unquestionably the less privileged in Society. That is the reality. The divide between black people is apparent in workplaces, where black people are sometimes used to invalidate discrimination or racism reports. For example, when the victim reports racism, the perpetrator is soon observed, attempting to work better with the next black person within the team to portray themselves to the contrary. Consequently, when the other black person is called upon to speak about their own experiences with such a perpetrator, they will immediately give guarded glowing feedbacks simply to safeguard their jobs or positions. Perpetrators can then walk free of any consequences and continue with the same behaviour, knowing that they will suffer no meaningful repercussions. Such a scenario enables racism to thrive persistently.

Another group of black people choose to disassociate themselves from race issues to avoid the associated emotional implications. This group prefer to focus on their jobs, and career growth, etc. which is understandable. However, it is essential to create some space to educate white people non-judgementally around racism without giving up too quickly.

Black Leaders and Managers should not take the "climbing ladder" off once they have climbed to a leadership position. They should mentor and support other black staff up the ladder and do so bravely and unapologetically.

This is because they are a disadvantaged group. Leaders should intentionally support skilled and well-deserving black colleagues to achieve their full potentials to fill positions of management and leadership. It will enable these staff to contribute to influencing positive change too. A leader or a manager's key role is to recognise skills and talents and ensure they are nurtured to their full potentials. Talent is not precluded to a specific group. Once you recognise skills and talent, flag them up and get others to join you to promote so that high workplace productivity is achieved. An environment of increased productivity is achieved through inclusion, supportiveness, and safety.

Black people must unite against a common goal and speak out in one voice against injustices to them and their colleagues in minority groups. They should strive to challenge racism constructively, knowing what battles to fight and what struggles to leave for another day.

Within this discourse, bravery is required; diplomacy is needed. Standing up for what is right with integrity is an excellent place to start. We should be bold in standing up for each other to achieve justice and fair play in the World.

Letter to Readers

Dear Readers,

I hope this letter meets you well.

I wanted to commiserate with you all concerning the tragic murder of George Floyd in the US in May 2020. This act, seen as an act of racism around the World, was a sore wound and heart-breaking for humanity. The incident affected us all whether we are of the black, brown, or white background. I could not watch the full eight-minute and forty-six-second video of the murder because of the distressing and deeply saddening nature. US President Joe Biden described the murder as a "knee on the neck of justice", and rightly so.

Agreeably, this murder is not an isolated incident because there were many before him and indeed more after him. These incidents have been ongoing for decades, not just in the US and the UK but in other European countries, etc.... covert and overt racism, systematic limitations, restrictions, and killings.

My fellow black social work, social care professionals and readers, hating racists is not the solution. It is about challenging racism constructively whilst providing education where required and as many times as needed.

My question to you is: How are you challenging racism? Are you challenging it, constructively? Do you strive to educate on anti-racism? Are you facilitating and supporting positive change?

My fellow white social work, social care professionals and readers, black people need the empathy of white people, their support and understanding around the issue of racism so that black lives can begin to matter too.

My question to you is: Are you consciously aware of your privileges? How are you embracing diversity and promoting inclusion? Are you facilitating and supporting positive change? Or are you obstructing change?

Summary

The benefits of diversity, the importance of preserving a person's identity and the need for cultural competence in social work and social care cannot be over-emphasized. As individuals, we cannot deny the prevalence of white privilege in Society. The murder of George Floyd has accentuated and brought some light to supposedly dark shaded areas and created more engagement with the Black Lives Matter (BLM) movement, and rightly so.

Social care staff, social workers, foster carers, public servants, politicians, etc., must pay more attention and discuss sensitive subjects like racism / conscious and unconscious bias. Ignorance is no longer an excuse. As earlier mentioned in this book, in late 2020 in the UK, the media reported a prominent public member, the FA Chairman, being forced to resign due to inappropriate language around diversity. Public servants, social care, social work professionals, and the public need to reframe their language. Language use must be purposeful and respect how individuals, groups, and communities choose to be identified.

In the humanitarian field of social work, lack of knowledge, understanding, and respect for service users' culture and beliefs is detrimental to the profession's ethos and could become costly. Social workers should engage positively with diversity, and their voices should be heard audibly advocating for Anti-racism and Equality. Social work is a profession that is fundamentally rooted in anti-oppressive and anti-discriminatory practice. Racism is a huge societal problem, and a lack of criticism can be deemed as complicity.

In early 2021, the Duke and Duchess of Sussex in England, Prince Harry, and Meghan, granted an interview with US talk show host Oprah Winfrey. The interview, which was watched by millions in the UK, US, and around the World, alluded to Meghan, the first mixed-race member of the Royal family in the UK, experiencing racism. The discussions showed that racial discrimination poses a clear and present danger in Society. It showed the impact that racism or the perception of racism can have on a person's emotional and mental wellbeing.

According to Meghan's admission, her mental health had deteriorated quite significantly, which is not an unfamiliar ground because racism harms people of colour deeply. It needs to be challenged and addressed right from the top, across institutional and leadership pipelines. Anti-racism education is critically required at all levels to support working positively with diversity. There needs to be a radical evolution to change the future narrative.

Following his inauguration as the 46th President of the United States of America, Joe Biden outlined his focus for the first 100 days in the office, which included plans to address racial inequality in the country. He stated: ***"This is the time to address systemic racism and inequity".*** Although this is coming decades too late, it may seem like a new dawn in the country and may hold some glimmer of hope… Joe Biden described the murder of George Floyd as ***"a knee on the neck of justice".*** This was an apt description that could not have been put any better. He further stated that addressing racial inequality was not a one department mission but indeed a whole Government department approach.

Likewise, it is safe to say that tackling inequality, systemic, or everyday racism in social care, the social work profession, and Society at large remains a whole community job. The struggle should not be only for those affected.

According to US President Joe Biden, ***"We are all God's Children; we should treat others as we like to be treated ourselves. All people are created equal and have a right to be treated equally".*** We are all indeed God's children…

"Systemic racism is corrosive, destructive and costly."

He further stated that it is time to let go of notions such as: ***"If you succeed I fail; If you get ahead, I fall behind; If you get the job, I lose mine and maybe worse of all, if I hold you down, I lift myself up.***

He concluded: ***When we lift each other up, we are all lifted up".***

Joe Biden effectively advocated for unity amongst diverse people and the embrace of diversity and inclusion in Society. His argument sums up this book.

"We are striving to forge our union with purpose. To compose a country committed to all cultures, colours, characters, and conditions of man" – Amanda Gorman, Inaugural Poet, US President Inauguration Jan 2021

I hope that I have used the VOT Diversity Acrostic Poem to convey a meaningful message around cultural competence. Social Work and Social care professionals must rewrite history to proffer well-rounded interventions in this revolving World of unprecedented and spectacular unknowns.

Reflection Notes

A true story that went viral on social media some time ago - Two five-year-old best friends, one black and one white, got the same hair cut to trick their teacher so she would not be able to tell them apart...?

No one is born racist

Reflection Notes

Decide to be a Culturally Sensitive Practitioner

Reflection Notes

I

Invite people to talk about their cultures, values, beliefs, and experiences

Reflection Notes

Value Client history, individuality, and differences

Reflection Notes

E - Explore client's realities, show curiosity

Reflection Notes

R - Reflect upon information and Knowledge received

Reflection Notes

S - Scrutinise yourself – Personal SWOT Analysis (Strengths, Weaknesses, Opportunities & Threats)

Reflection Notes

I - Identify strategies to aid your work

Reflection Notes

T

T - Train yourself to treat people and families individually

Reflection Notes

Y - Yield to culturally sensitive practice

Professionals feedback

'Diversity Acrostic Poem creatively acronymises the word diversity and effectively draws out some of the key principles of cultural sensitivity' - Wayne Reid, Professional Officer, The British Association of Social Workers (BASW).

'The Acrostic poem is a creative way of finding the simplicity in the complexity of diversity. It will be a useful tool to encourage cultural awareness' - Siobhan Maclean, Social Work Publisher - Kirwin Maclean.

'Diversity Acrostic Poem book is not only timely and innovative; it is also refreshingly inspiring, bold and challenges. Thank you for writing this book. I look forward to having it and would encourage everyone to read it' - Ellen Holroyd, Social Work Practitioner Surrey.

'The book is written with passion, the Diversity Poem is a great working tool, and there are some real gems of wisdom' – Jill Seeney, Children's book Author & Fostering Development Manager WSCC.

'This book is an insightful and inspiring read that reflects on racism and diversity in a humane and creative way. The Diversity Acrostic Poem gives Social Work Practitioners a helpful tool to use in tackling the inequalities many of the people we work with face every day in our unequal society' - Adrian Rutledge, Social Work Practice Manager, WSCC.

'Diversity Acrostic poem is an example of creative anti-racist social work practice. Racism and white privilege are perpetuated through division, paralysis, and avoidance. Vivian's work challenges us not to turn away but to rise up and engage, with ourselves, with each other and with children and their families. Her work manages to be simple, inclusive, and playful – it is an invitation to social work to be curious and creative. In her performance of the poem at a CoramBAAF practice forum, Vivian skillfully mobilized her insight, vulnerability, and energy. It felt like a gift to us. I am sure social work colleagues will appreciate her work and her challenge' - Louise Sims, Kinship Care and Fostering Consultant CoramBAAF

'Vivian's work on the issue of diversity and anti-racist Social Work is inspiring and timely… so many parallels with what

is going on across the world and such a powerful tool to use' – Yewukai Tsanga, Group Manager, Children Looked After.

'This book presents one of the most helpful explanations on diversity. It is filled with examples and strategies to assist social work professionals and clinicians. It is highly recommended' - Elaine Williams, Independent Senior Social Work Practitioner.

'The Diversity Acrostic Poem Book is a creative and interesting approach to addressing the issue of diversity, inclusion and racism. The presentation and writing style is easy to read. The book aims to challenge social work practitioners, policymakers and the readers in general about the issue of social graces and the importance of diversity, equity and inclusion as a means of creating equal opportunities for practitioners and the children and families that we work within social care. It showcases a creative way of entering a dialogue about ensuring that people from diverse background are offered the opportunity to share their ideas, perspectives and feel respected and appreciated. Toyin Sokale, Children Looked After Practice Manager.

About the Author

Vivian Okeze-Tirado is a Senior Social Worker and a Practice Educator for West Sussex County Council. She sat as a Social Work Member of the Adoption Panel for two years. Vivian facilitates Social Work training to Social Work Practitioners and Foster Carers on the Secure Base Model, Diversity, Cultural Competence & Black Lives Matter, etc. Vivian's first degree was in Linguistics, followed by a Masters' degree in Business Administration - Management. Having sufficiently explored her initial career, Vivian decided to move sideways to Social Work to pursue a more humanitarian career around improving the outcomes for vulnerable children and families. Vivian obtained her second Masters' degree in Social Work from Brighton University in 2014. Vivian is keen on Social Work research and practice development. She has developed useful materials for Social Workers and Foster Carers to enhance the experiences of children from all backgrounds. Vivian is the author of *Diversity Acrostic Poem and Book.* The poem is also published in the British Association of Social Workers (BASW) book. *Outlanders: Hidden Narratives from Social Workers of Colour - an anthology.* As a Social Worker of African origin, a wife and a mum, Vivian understands the importance of Cultural Competence in Social Work. She advocates strongly for Justice and Equality

Practical Help and Support for the Less Privileged

https://redefineshop.co.uk/

https://blacklivesmatter.com/

https://berrywell.org.uk/

https://www.childline.org.uk/

https://www.nspcc.org.uk/

https://www.unicef.org.uk/

https://www.actionforchildren.org.uk/

Useful Resources

Books

Alko, Selina. ***The Case for Loving: The Fight for Interracial Marriage*** Arthur A. Levine Books 2015.

Brooks, Felicity. ***All about Families.*** Usborne Publishing, 2018.

Byers, Grace. ***I am enough.*** HarperCollins, 2020.

Di Angelo Robin. ***White Fragility. Why it's so hard for White People to talk about racism.*** Allen Lane, Britain, 2018.

Eddo-Lodge Reni. ***Why I'm no longer talking to White People About Race.*** Bloomsbury Publishing, 2018.

Guyton Hunt, Imelda. ***Black Culture traditions – Visible and Invisible.*** Cognella Inc 2020.

Hakim, Adi. ***Black British History. New Perspectives.*** Zed Books Illustrated 2019.

Harrison, Vashti. ***Little Leaders. Bold Women in Black History.*** Penguin Random House, 2017.

Holton, Lois. ***A History of African American People.*** Wayne State University Press 1997.

Johnson, Leah. ***You Should See Me in a Crown.*** Scholastic Corporation, 2020.

Katz, Karen, ***The Colors of us.*** Square Fish, 2002.

Lester, Julius. ***Let's talk about race.*** Harper Coll; Reprint edition 2020.

Lewis Denise and Awolaja Flora. ***Black Children in Care: Health, Hair & Skin.*** Positive Image project Ltd 2014.

Lindsay, Ben. ***We need to talk about Race. Understanding the Black Experience in White Majority Churches.*** Society for Promoting Christian Knowledge 2019.

Love, Jessica. ***Julian is a Mermaid.*** Walker Books Ltd, 2018.

Memory, Jelani. ***A Kid's book about racism. Kids Book About,*** Incorporated, A, 2019.

Oluo, Ijeoma. ***So, You Want to Talk About Race.*** Basic Books, 2018.

Reid, W & Maclean S. Outlanders: ***Hidden Narratives from Social Workers of Colour.*** BASW England, Kirwin Maclean Associates 2021.

Saad, Layla & Di Angelo Robin. ***Me and White Supremacy: How to Recognise Your Privilege, Combat Racism, and Change the World.*** Quercus 2020.

Sissay, Lemn. ***My Name is Why.*** Canongate Books Ltd, 2019.

Thompson, N. Promoting Equality: ***Working with Diversity and Difference.*** 3rd edition. Palgrave Macmillan, 2011.

Torrey, Maldonado. ***What Lane?*** *Penguin Random House, 2020.*

Bibliography

Books

Boyne, John (2006). *The boy in the striped pyjamas*. Vintage Children's Classics; 1st edition.

Brown, K. and Rutter, L. (2008). *Critical Thinking for Social Work*. Exeter, Learning Matters.

Burnham, J. (2012) *Developments in Social GRRRAAACCEEESSS:* visible – invisible and voiced – unvoiced. In I.-B. Krause (ed.) Culture and Reflexivity in Systemic Psychotherapy: Mutual Perspectives (pp. 139–160). London: Karnac

Di Angelo, R. (2018) *White fragility -Why it's so hard for white people to talk about racism*. Allen Lane

Lindsay, B. (2019) *We need to talk about race. Understanding the black experience in white-majority churches.* Society for Promoting Christian Knowledge

Miller, W. & Rollnick, S. (2002) *Motivational Interviewing: Preparing people for change.* 2nd edition. New York: Guilford Press.

Moon, J. A. (2004). *A Handbook of Reflective and Experiential Learning: Theory and practice.* Routledge Falmer.

Schon, D. (1983). *The Reflective Practitioner.* How professionals think in action. London: Temple Smith.

Siegel, D. (2010). *The Mindful Therapist: A Clinician's Guide to Mindsight and Neural Integration. New York: W. W. Norton & Company*

Thompson, N. (2006). *Anti-Discriminatory Practice. London, Palgrave Macmillan, 2006,*

Thompson, S. and Thompson, N. (2008). *The Critically Reflective Practitioner.* Basingstoke: Palgrave, Macmillan

Thompson, N. (2009). *Practicing Social Work. Meeting the professional challenge.* Palgrave Macmillan.

Thompson, N. (2012). *Anti – Discriminatory Practice.* 5th edition. Palgrave Macmillan.

Websites

https://www.basw.co.uk/system/files/resources/PCF%20Final%20Documents%20Overview%2011%20June%202018.pdf (Professional Capabilities Framework Domains)

https://www.basw.co.uk/media/news/2020/jul/social-graces-practical-tool-address-inequality

https://www.communitycare.co.uk/2020/10/30/food-marker-identity-supporting-foster-childrens-cultural-heritage/

https://www.communitycare.co.uk/2011/02/25/promoting-diversity-in-social-work-practice-to-combat-oppression/

https://corambaaf.org.uk/sites/default/files/Catalogues/Fostering%20CoramBAAF%20Catalogue.pdf

https://www.education-ni.gov.uk/

https://www.equalityhumanrights.com/en/equality-act

https://www.gov.uk/government/organisations/department-for-education

https://www.legislation.gov.uk/ukpga/2010/15/section/4
Equality Act 2010

https://onlinesocialwork.vcu.edu/blog/cultural-competence-in-social-work/

https://www.researchinpractice.org.uk/children/publications/2017/july/confident-practice-with-cultural-diversity-frontline-briefing-2017/

https://www.skillsforcare.org.uk/Leadership-management/developing-leaders-and-managers/Supporting-the-diverse-workforce-within-adult-social-care.aspx#WebinarSeries

https://sites.uea.ac.uk/providingasecurebase/the-secure-base-model

https://www.socialworkengland.org.uk/

https://www.youtube.com/watch?v=h7mzj0cVL0Q
Deconstructing White Privilege with Dr Di Angelo

https://vottraining.co.uk

Thank you for reading this book.